CARLA

CARLO

Carla
Carla Woodburn

Leamington Books
Edinburgh

ISBN 9781914090561

Published by Leamington Books
32 Leamington Terrace
Edinburgh, Scotland

Carla Ambigram by John Langdon
Design by Cavan Convery
Set in Baskerville and Bebas
Production by Peter Burnett
Printed by Imprint Digital, Exeter

leamingtonbooks.com/carla

I am the daughter of Woody Woodburn and Kathleen Munro and I dedicate this book to them both as a thank you for bringing me into this world and supporting me through the years, sadly my father Woody real name Rodrick passed away in 2011. My mother Kathy is a great support for me and without her I wouldn't know the encouragement she regularly gives me.

I dedicate this book to both my parents and thank them for their love.

CONTENTS

In this book you will find a collection of my poetry written over a lifetime up until now. I'm currently 39 and some of these poem's date back to my teenage years; some are more recent.

I'm from a small town in the highlands of Scotland called Tain where I lived until I was 19 before moving to Glasgow, chasing city life and a bright future. I've enjoyed poetry and written poetry all my years, having found the passion when I was in primary school and poetry is something I've never put down. In my early 20's I wrote a lot of poetry in private, never sharing with people other than family members and annoying my friends with them, regularly asking, "do you want to hear another poem?" I lived in Glasgow up until I was 26, enjoying the party lifestyle that Glasgow had to offer. I then moved to Barcelona and got involved with many things, one being the Barcelona Poetry Workshop where I attended weekly poetry meetings and jointly released a group anthology, Together and Apart my first publication. It was in Barcelona where my confidence for poetry grew. I returned to Glasgow four years later I was ready to start attending poetry events and immersed myself in the Glasgow poetry scene, where I found Tell It Slant poetry bookshop and where I organised and hosted my own monthly events as part of Tell It Slant poetry bookshop, Express Yourself. I then started my own poetry radio show with Sunny

Govan Radio and called the radio show Express Yourself too.

The poems in this book are inspired by life, spirituality and fun and family. I enjoy making something from simple everyday things and creating poetry.

ME

Am a Heilan lass,
Born an bred,
Just like the coo,
A Heilan bairn of the toon of Tain.
A tattie lover and planter,
Fae the fields.
My ma n da they taught me weel,
Thaymselves fae Glesga dwellings.
They didnae ken their daughter widnae blether
wae the same Glesga tunin.
I wis born a Heilan lass,
Played the bagpipes in class.
Jumped the hay bales and dry grass.
Kin talk like a teuchter if asked.
Albeit a bit mare Glesga as time passed.
A moved tae the city in my later teens,
Fur city life I wis keen,
The breght lights and aww the dancin,
Fancied my chancin so's a did,
Took masel a gallivantin.
But through aw my years,
Only wan passion sincere
Wis my poetry n ma music,
which av awis held dear.
In aw tongues in which we speak,
Gaelic, Doric, Scots, slang fae the street,
Wheriver ye be,

Let yer tongue gang free,
And lang live Scots leid ae poetry.

WITH AND WITHOUT

Like without liking anything,
care without caring.
love without care,
and care without love,
and like without like.
sex without emotion,
tenderness without touch,
lick without saliva,
gentle but rough.
Joy without tears,
and tears without joy,
heart without breaking,
heart not a toy.
Smile without interest,
tears without tears,
laughter at wrong moments,
fears without fear.
Strong without strength,
empty when full,
scared when the light is on,
and dark under the moon.
Warmth when it's toasty,
cheese toasty in bed,
mind games with the mindless,
stressful when restful.
Weak at the knees,
double jointed and bendy,
mobile home built for a Wendy.

HE & SHE

Mr & Mrs,
husband & Wife,
this is my spouse,
this is my trouble and strife.
She wears the trousers,
he wears the marigolds,
she never does anything,
he does what he's told.
He keeps her stable,
she drives him wild,
he helps her financially,
and she feeds his appetite.
He helps her leave parties when she's had too much
to drink,
he hates when she beats him at farting,
hers always stink.
She makes him tea and he makes her laugh,
he loves it when he comes home from work and
she's run his bath.
He likes the massage and she loves the body
contact,
she watches Netflix and he pays the contract.
He's very strong and she's strong too,
she's loves his arms wrapped round her,
and he loves the boobs.
He watches football and she loves the poetry,
he wants her mind and she wants him emotionally.

16

He likes chilli and she likes garlic,
he says hot and she says Baltic,
black is white and white is black,
she loves him & he loves her back.

POWER, PEN, SWORD, YOUR WORD

What is more powerful?
The pen?
The sword?
Your word?
I'd like to believe what I've heard.
Not nonsense.
Not shite.
Is what you say right?
Because I can write a mighty fine line,
And with a sword I'll cut you down to size.
What is mightier I ask you.
What?

DAMN YOU SCOTLAND

Damn you Scotland in the winter,
You make me fucking shiver,
You make me want malt whisky,
And I'm always fucking frisky.
My tights are 200 denier,
And my scarf is wool and my cheeks are red,
Got my lecky blanket on in bed,
I love you Scotland
You're the best,
Even though my nipples are constantly erect.

CABLES AND LEADS

Let's not get our wires crossed,
because let's face it,
we have quite a lot of loose wires kicking about,
and continuously buying more,
adding to our collection of chargers,
adapter leads,
jacks to phonos,
kettle blooming leads,
cables, HDMIs,
if I don't charge my iPhone the battery dies.
USBs,
and even more memory sticks.
My house is a technophobe's worst nightmare.
Batteries that last no longer than 4 hours,
so, we need yet another lead,
as an energy feed,
a separate power pack to feed my need,
at the least so I can sit in bed with my Kindle and
read.
My whole life I have been haunted by cables and
wires,
and it's only getting worse
As evolution introduces us with more toys with
powers,
I'm even smoking a cigarette that needs charged
via my laptop,
this now is the only way I smoke,

20

and yet again it has its own power cable,
and if that battery runs out, I'm not nicotine stable.
This is cracking me up,
it's a new rucksack I need to carry around all these
cables and leads,
and power sources,
I'm beginning to feel like my own personal power
plant.
But I need a lead-free house,
wireless really is not wireless is it...

A WINDOW TO THE HEART

Don't believe all that you read,
looks can deceive,
don't believe all you perceive.
Through this window that I built for you,
to peep through,
there are many decorations,
hanging mobiles,
a dream catcher,
and stained glass,
shining reds and greens that light up the wall,
I even threw in a mirror so you could see your
reflection,
this is its beauty.

DOES IT FIT?

I was the Princess at the ball,
I wore my glass slippers,
and one fell off because it was slightly over sized,
I'm not perfect,
it's possible one foot is bigger than the other.
You should see my sisters!
They were cheap glass slippers anyway...
My Prince,
he had been watching me for some time,
he doesn't know me,
so, he doesn't know the pleasure I get from him
watching me.
I think he knows I'm shy.
The clock struck home time,
and as charming as ever he was.
I could hardly speak,
my cloth quickly turning to rags in front of his
eyes.
My pumpkin arrived,
ashamed and shy,
I galloped off.
I think I left my heart behind.
I hope he finds it and it fits.

BARCELONA – A MASTER'S PEACE

In a city raised as a tomb of crystal,
You would think we were going to see the Wizard
of Oz,
Shards as sharp as the blade of a knife,
Rip through the city openings,
Now named as streets or in Spanish, calles,
and forming barrios.
Should be emerald green,
But shines so crystal clear that the sun reflects
from every window.
Narrow openings positioned perfectly,
To the stars and the moon, and the sunbeams.
These give me a perfect view.
And in every crystal, there is deception,
this city has that too.
It is more than a city,
but a graveyard.
The city is a masterpiece.
Here lies the perfect monument,
All you need to do is open your eyes and see.

THERE IS A CLOWN IN TOWN

There's a clown in town,
he sent me an email and asked me out on a date.
I feel strange to have a clown as a mate.
He takes great pride in his clown like attire,
He sent me a bunch of water squirting flowers.

There's a clown in town and he wants to be my
friend.
He wears bright red plastic shoe that bend.
He's got one of those honky red noses,
he's as clumsy as they come,
I suppose he's...
got lots of other clown friends,
a group of clowns clowning around,
and he's asked me out on a date,
he wants to be my friend,
my mate.

There's a clown in town and he's always clowning
around,
telling jokes and conjuring tricks,
stripey green and red trousers and walking on huge
stilt sticks.
Welcome in any circus,
he hurts himself on purpose.
He attends all these clown events,
trousers so big he's wearing a tent,

and he's got those big clown pants,
drives about in a flowery painted clown car,
he takes his clown image extremely far.

There's a clown in town and he wants to date me,
I'm a little weirded out,
my life's clown free.
His face is disguised because of the makeup he
wears,
his honky red nose and he's got green hair.
There's a clown in town that I feel weird about,
this clown he wants to take me out.

SUNKEN SHIP

Looking at your sunken ship,
I want to dive into your wreckage,
as I know your treasures are hidden deep,
deep within the waters,
the murky waters of the River Clyde.
So still does the water sit,
So much darkness there mixed in with it.
A shipwreck just waiting to be discovered
and your true glory uncovered.
As I dive deep and vision blind,
who knows what treasures I will find?
A pirate would have left a trap,
but you my love left a treasure map.
So cold this water,
vision thick with scum,
I can't believe I'm the only one,
to discover what I have found,
lurking in the underground.
Your treasures can never be worn nor seen,
but I know their worth
because I have been.

EQUALITY

What did you have for dinner last night?
They feed me well in the soup kitchen.
They feed me well from the food bank.
Thank you for sending your price parcels,
They fed my child,
but we are still looking for clean water to drink,
I beg of you,
and I thank you.
No gays allowed,
it will not be tolerated,
it goes against our religious beliefs,
and you cannot have an abortion,
we do not care about your needs.
Only black people,
only white people,
ONLY PEOPLE!
I cannot be your friend because I am vain,
you have ginger hair and glasses
and I'm still acting like I did when I was ten.
Vote for me,
vote for him,
get involved or drop out of society,
become a drop-out because we are forcing this upon
you.
Make your choice now as this is what you have to do.
There are laws enforced against your freedom of
speech,

because we cannot have people listening to the
diversity you teach.
And because of the way your mind works,
we will label you,
we will push you to the side as if your no more
than a babbling fool.
Oh, I like your designer trainers,
you're so cool.
I wore Dunlops to school.
WAR! What is it good for?
Absolutely nothing!
I see you begging at the side of the street so tonight
you can eat.
You cannot work because your parents crippled
you when you were younger,
and for this purpose alone,
So you can beg to bring money home.
It saddens me.
And now,
in a world so full of diversity,
I ask you,
what exactly is equality?

CHAUFFEUR DRIVEN

You see what they want you to see,
the ones who think they control you and me.
The puppeteers,
the men with strings,
those who wear the pinkie rings.
The knights of the round table.
Those who keep our world stable.
The men in suits and polished boots,
counting cash to distribute.
Chauffeur driven,
shielded from the rain,
never felt a pine of pain.
The aristocrats,
the top cats,
the gentlemen who wear top hats.
With gout and shiny red nose,
Wives showing off their well-manicured toes,
that's where all the money goes.

THE GUIDE

In the calm of the night,
when it's only me and the moonlight.
When your friends have all gone home,
you turn the music off, or the TV, and turn off
your phone.
You're sitting in silence and alone.
When the shadows are your only companion,
and you can clearly hear your mind.
Relaxing to the sight of the overhead light.
Slight strain on the eyes because it's so bright.
You use this time,
you reflect on your day,
you file things away,
in your mind.
You pray a secret prayer to your guide.
You know there's no one standing next to you
because you can't see them,
but you feel a presence by your side.

CHASING MY FAIRY-TALE

It was the wind in the willow that brought you to
my pillow.
Thumbelina so small,
but grew when she met you.
And when I walked through the wardrobe,
I entered into a whole new world,
with you around.
And like Mary Poppins,
my feet have not touched the ground.
And like The Mermaid I'm chasing my fairy-tale,
I'd throw down my brunette locks if I thought it
would help you climb to my tower,
and with you in my bed I'd hope for many
mattresses,
and I promise,
I would never look at another gingerbread man
again.

AN AMBIVALENT STRUCTURE

The structure was ambivalent,
with many points of view,
looking through a mirror glass of speculation was
what one had to do.
Taking in each angle of the structure,
each glance altering the scene,
it was the most ambiguous structure I had ever
seen.
Much like an optical illusion,
reflecting symmetry on each point,
hard to reach conclusion,
concluding what you want.

YESTERDAY THEY KILLED FIFTY

Yesterday they killed fifty.
Innocent lives went to waste,
dancing in the name of love,
in what was supposed to be a peaceful place.
Today the world showed up in colour,
in a protest in the name of peace.
They are killing people every month,
there is bloodshed on the streets.
Yesterday they killed fifty,
a mother shed tears for her son,
the action of another human,
and the inhumanity from a gun.

THE TALE OF A FEMALE

Hell hath no fury like a woman scorned,
every man knows and has been warned,
with rage and strength in her eyes,
hell mend you if you make her cry.
The female of the species is more deadly than the
male,
it be told in many a tale,
the lady is not for turning,
and will send a philanderer packing and quickly
running.
So, it be right to approach with caution,
when you see her temper quickly blossom,
because when her eyes turns red it's time to go,
as every man should duly know.

ALL IN A DAY'S WORK

rules and measurements,
measuring to scale,
rulers and calculators,
mathematics,
decimal points,
percentages.

ANGEL

So angelic,
With a sweet tooth,
and able to deceive with a flutter of her wings,
and sometimes mischievous,
because she likes fun.
And it's easy to wash the dirt from her angelic face,
dust off the wings and take flight.

DEAR BODY

Dear body,
I'm sorry,
I've neglected you over the years,
My own neglect brings me to tears.
Not much I regret,
But I regret one thing,
Not putting you at the front of the queue for
everything.

Dear body,
It's been a long time of abuse,
Thanks for being strong while I've been obtuse.
And you hold your own when I can be distant,
Your reliable when I'm hesitant.

Sorry body,
For whenever I've put you in situations you don't
care for,
Or situations you wouldn't dare to,
But thank you,
I love you,
Were both still alive.
We've come this far together,
Still friends and survived.
We've rattled some cages,
We've sprained and bruised,
Been adored and been used,

But dear body,
It's always been me and you.
From my soul,
To my heart,
To my brain in my head,
My lips mutter the words my bodies already heard.
I thank you from my toes to my fingertips,
My womanly hips.
I thank you for your support,
And these fine legs,
Our smile,
Our eyes in which we cast view,
I thank you for helping me through.

Dear body,
You're the best.
You've always been my friend,
Till death do us party till the end.

RED WINE FRIENDS

Lost in a wine glass,
her lips stained with red,
her glass smeared in red wax,
Lipstick taints her glass,
red wine taints her mind.
Lost in the wine glass,
there is nothing for her left to find.
She downs bottle after cheese after bottle after
cheese,
she thinks this makes things better,
but a moment on the lips,
forever the hiccups.
She corks another bottle,
Three down two more to go,
the room is her tomb,
the glass her only friend,
her lipstick not the only thing that's making her a
lush.

BLUE BIRD

Hello little blue bird,
how do you sit today?
You little blue tit.
Twittering away like a real twit.
You're making it,
making a distracting noise from my silence,
little blue tit,
little bird.
And why they call you blue when you are clearly
grey or brown,
I'll never know,
maybe you were feeling blue the day we named
you,
Little blue tit,
we all feel blue from time to time,
How do you sit today?
Little blue tit.

LEST WE FORGET

When you forget the rhymes,
the poetry,
the motion of the rhythm,
the structure and the words,
you get something that doesn't really fit in at all,
a word long,
a sequence small.
Absurd.
Then if you think of yourself on a spiral staircase,
with twists and turns,
you can take your poetry anywhere,
Like a Salvador Dali painting,
a mirror tunnel,
or a kaleidoscope.
You can be an eagle soaring through the sky at one
hundred miles an hour,
you can be an hour glass,
with a perfect hour glass figure.

ONE DAY, BUT NOT IN ONE DAY

One day,
and I don't know what day,
but one day,
I'll find my place,
my grace,
stop standing on my loose lace.
One day,
I don't know what day,
I'll choose my path,
a different path,
a satisfying path,
a gratifying path.
One day I'll get that dream job I try so hard for but
fail.
One day I'll stop chasing my tail,
my tail that doesn't exist,
one day I'll find the power to resist what is.
One day I'll make my way to home,
but not all in one day.

EVERYONE IS EQUAL IN HOSPITAL

Corridors of trolley wheels feel of steel
contraptions,
Medical equipment has never looked so un-
tantalising.
All shiny and sterile,
and threatening.
Wet wipes with no thrill labels,
plastic caps,
plastic taps,
clear plastic water dispensers with plastic cups on
sterile plastic tables.
Easy wiped,
mopped,
disinfected and floors reflected,
the blue gowns and trolley wheels,
and the pissed off faces from the people's feels.
The days turns to nights and the nights turns to
rays,
sectioned up with medication breaks and three
meals a day.
Institutionalised,
and you're surrounded with sick tired people and
sad eyes,
everyone is equal in hospital.

THE MAGPIE POEM

The magpies have lost their home,
They're cutting down the trees.
The tree surgeon did not care at all,
He's done it out of greed.
I see the members of the crow family,
So vilified.
Steeped in superstition.
Looking for once where was nest,
Now sad beaked bird,
Its home it must be missing.
Daily they arrive,
In double figures,
I salute them like Sergeant Biggers,
And admire their long-tailed figures.
With such a reputation,
Curious and inquisitive,
This common pretty bird,
Is anything but primitive.
Provoking such strong views,
Some love them,
Some don't.
Their chattering away,
Can be hauntingly taunting.
Its home it must be wanting.
Misunderstood,
Elegant shimmering of iridescence,
I love the nature of this bird,

And it's highly social presence.
Flashes of slick petrol blue,
Sheen on feathers with green gloss slithers,
Little stubby wings,
It's said they'll steel your diamond rings.
Scavengers of the sky,
Opportunists,
Omnivorous,
Eating anything of the kind,
Be sure to salute the magpie,
If it's only one that you find.

LATEX

Latex was made for me and you,
It was invented for us,
to squeeze into.
And rub my body with your latex glove of love,
before we make latex Love.
You love me in the latex scud.
Latex was made for me and you,
I'm sure!
Your latex mat that I sat on,
and would pretend I was your latex pussy cat,
Latex spray,
And my black shimmering wet body.
This was made for us.
The body suction gave you an erection,
and I sucked you off.
We used black latex condoms as protection,
I licked your latex,
and now I ask you to pull me from this latex skin,
I've grown so accustomed to sitting in.

BLOOD RED LIPSTICK

Blood red lipstick drips from your swollen Botox
lips,
like the gloss you use has been abused,
it smears down your face because you wiped your
face with your arm,
I must admit it adds a certain glam,
You have the same smear on your face as you have
on your arm.
Your false eyelash is stuck to your face,
And the sink that you sit on might break,
But luckily you don't weigh much,
You're underweight.
As I put my mascara on with you,
and my makeup is not picture perfect too.
We are girls and I respect you!

MAN MACHINE

He is half man and half machine,
he has the best dick you've ever seen.
He goes down low and in-between and when he
puts it in me my face just beams.
He hits all the right spots,
he loves to put his hands on my bott,
He works my body when I'm on top,
and he doesn't want me to stop,
He pleasures me until I want him to stop.
He sends me electric impulses to my brain,
he gives me orgasms that are just insane,
he is half man and half machine,
he's so fit,
so muscley,
so fit and lean.
He takes me and spins me round,
he likes it best when my feet aren't on the ground,
yes,
My body's bound.
He is half man and half machine,
he can even give me orgasms in my dreams,
even his voice sounds so right,
He makes my belly all tingly
I rub my toes together and my legs go tight.

BUNNY GIRL

His name is Harry and he is funny,
he employs me to be his bunny.
All he wants is for me to bounce around,
with my bunny tail,
on the ground.
Sometimes I do want to play,
and take off my bunny clothes,
in a sexy way.
My name is Harry and you are funny,
and now you are indeed my bunny.

IF I COULD FIX A BROKEN HEART

If I could fix a broken heart,
Id stick it back with glue,
but fixing broken hearts is not such an easy thing
to do.
If I could fix a broken heart I'd open up a shop,
I'd be fixing broken hearts all day as I'm   sure
there are a lot.
Some like shattered mirrors,
some simply cracked in half,
If I could fix a broken heart I'd open up a class.
If I could fix a broken heart,
I wouldn't charge a lot,
I'm sure I'd earn a fortune,
the demand is high,
It's the only heart we've got.
I'd reinforce broken hearts,
so, they never broke again,
the words 'broken heart' would never mean the
same.
So, if you've got a broken heart don't think that it's
all bad,
I know you feel the pain and you're feeling kind of
sad,
I don't have all the answers,
Apparently, time heals all wounds,

I am no doctor,
I'm just a girl,
Your broken heart heals soon.

RADICAL

What does it mean to me?
my own radicality.
I am this amazing thing in my own way,
I do try to do something fear provoking every day,
my ideas regularly, they scare me.
But I don't think that's what makes something
radical.
It's a lot of pressure maintaining this stature.
A quality gained through growth, development and
achievement.
I am innovative and this poem is clearly about me.
And the ways I see myself.
What started as an idea for a poem suddenly felt
so personal,
Like the whole nature was based on my grandeur,
me
and I find it hard to put into words,
my personality.
Regularly shaking the foundation with new ideas,
that's me.
A gift of a curse,
I'll wear it like a shiny new purse.
I could talk about the time I woke up in the
Highlands of Scotland,
By the end of the day, I had moved away.
Compulsion.
Impulsive.

Reactive like an atom bomb.
A revolutionary decision in my life choices,
One I didn't have to give much thought to,
or at least not for long.
Some of the best ideas are the ones that scare you,
but we show no fear.
That is radical to me.

Who's the most radical person I know,
It's my mother.
My mother invented me,
She's radical too, see.

And in these radical times,
we call upon radical ideas,
we think radical thoughts and have radical   fears.
Radical things happen,
progression itself is radical

How could I not be?
Radical,
What does it mean to me?
I've never defined myself as anything,
but I'm aware,
Radical is in my nature.
I'm aware if I make changes,
they are radical,
a radical change in direction
I made a radical intervention.
Radical is what I am because of what I've been
through,

where I came from,
what it took for me to get to where I am now,
my striving to better myself,
my striving to make something of myself,
And here I am,
full health,
no wealth in poetry,
an abundance of words,
and a voice that is my wealth,
this is my wealth.

MOULDY SOUP

The soup's gone mouldy because I left it out
overnight,
I didn't eat it because it didn't look right,
it had a layer of skin and was a bit condensed,
so, I had a dinner party and I fed it to my friends.
Anyway, I think I missed out because they all said
it was great,
I said there wasn't enough for me to have a plate.
The next thing I know they all got high,
was there a drug involved?
Penicillin,
My soup has evolved.
Then they want the recipe and what do I say,
Oh, I'm sorry you ate my soup that was left for
some days,
so, I kept my recipe,
my crème de la crème,
and every now and again I have a giggle when I
feed it to my friends.

SHE SWALLOWED A SPIDER

I once knew a woman who swallowed a spider,
so, I could re-release the poem of how it tickled inside her.
She allowed me to document as she dropped it into her latch,
but three days later another 1000 babies did hatch.
Like something from a horror, the spiders emerged,
from every orifice she had the spiders did surge.
They took over her house and they terrorised her kids,
I could only watch as I was documenting this.

The spiders were possessive and took to her like a mum,
as she continued to give birth to spider 1001.

Her husband returned from an overseas trip,
to see his wife mothering these spiders instead of their kids.
A noble man he tried to remain calm as he sat on his couch,
but these possessive spiders they wanted him out.
They'd congregate like an army,
and bite him any chance they got,
getting anywhere near his wife was now a far distant thought.
He needed a plan to get these spiders out of his life,

he longed for the closeness of his kids and his
wife.
He had a solution and he had a goal,
he was getting his wife back by pest control.

Pest control arrived,
another scary sight I might add,
all those hoses,
and fumigation tubes and other equipment he had.
The wife looked excited because she too wanted
these spiders out,
and have faith in the pest control guy as he was
sexy and stout.
Out comes his hoses and he fumigated her body,
whilst the husband waited loyally outside in the
lobby.

Spiders all gone and one happy wife,
who swallowed the spider for the tickle inside her?

THE HORSIEMOUSIE AND THE HIPPOSAUR

The Horsiemousie and the Hipposaur
having tea and scones at the table,
when the Hipposaur says to the Horsiemousie,
"You should be in the stable!"

Horsiemousie replies: "But why should I be in a
stable when I've the body of a mouse,
when you're a Hipposaur and you're sitting in my
house?"

IF YOU THINK ABOUT IT

We are a million different people in one smile,
We are a million different lifestyles in one style,
our reflections stay the same,
but our memories change,
our skin ages but our soul is preserved,
our actions always being observed by ourselves.
We are an attitude from day to day,
we are a house in which we choose to stay.
We are a moment in someone else's life,
and loved by people we don't even know loves us.
We are emotions running high and low,
Lost pedestrians looking for the correct way to go,
mystified humans,
mystifying about life and what could be,
we are what could be described as a mere speck of
dust in a vast space oddity.
Our intellect and dialect,
In our eyes are never perfect,
We seek advancement in all we do,
Never satisfied with what we already knew.
Captivated by things like fear, love, lust and hate,
we are someone else's fate waiting to be met.
We are our own gambling addiction,
judging on our own lives how much we want to
bet.
Tears drop down our cheeks of joy and sadness,
celebrations or regret.
We group together in packs to laugh out loud,

our body clocks determine when our bodies bow out.
Blood pumping through our physique keeping us active,
Plastering on makeup and moisturisers to keep us attractive.
As a race,
highly interactive.
Exchanging bodily fluids by the connecting of two bodies and souls through the action of love making,
creating babies in the womb to keep creating.
Building.
Demolishing,
planting and erecting.
Our motto,
If at first you don't succeed keep on perfecting.

HEART OF STONE

Heart of stone,
too hard to carve,
too big to sit with,
useless.

No chiselling,
no cracking,
no altering this heart of stone.
So cold and grey I think it might rain,
this heart of stone feels no pain.

No blood will seep from this heart of stone,
you cannot get blood from a stone,
it's too hard to carve,
too big to sit with,
useless.

I throw the heart on the ground,
only to hear the heart pound,
there is no chip,
there is no dent,
there is no blood that seeps from this heart of
stone,
you cannot get blood from a stone.
It's too hard to carve,
too big to sit with,
useless.

TECHNOLOGY AND THE NEIGHBOURS

Technology and the neighbours,
fuck the peace,
disturb the peace.

Put technology in first gear,
there is no war here,
No war here!
What a carry on,
the neighbours only like one song,
Fuck the peace
Disturb the peace,
Bring it on!!
What it brings you fear,
I've put technology in first gear,
Bring your body over to hear.
What you trying to say?
NO WAY.
Don't beat about the bush,
Come, Play.

Technology and the neighbours,
fuck the peace,
disturb the peace all the way.

I'm no karaoke machine you know,
Playing you requests,
IN YOUR DREAMS.

In your dreams you hear the noise of war and it
brings you fear,
put technology in first gear,
fuck the peace,
disturb the peace.

PISS OFF I'M NOT TELLING YOU

Who I love,
I don't know,
I know it's a guy,
P.O.I.N.T.Y.
Tall not small,
Sweet but mean to keep me keen.
An equal balance,
I love a challenge,
don't as why,
P.O.I.N.T.Y.
Brown hair's nice and I do like blonde,
Everyone's eyes are nice,
green brown or blue,
who is the guy?
P.O.I.N.T.Y.

JUST A GIRL

Just a girl with a plate,
okay, maybe lots of plates,
just a girl spinning lots of plates,
some are late.
Just a girl spinning lots of plates,
remembering to spin the late ones,
just a girl with all the plates spinning.
Cooking up a storm in the kitchen.
Just a girl spinning lots of plates,
with her fingers in a lot of pies,
just a girl spinning lots of plates with pies on them,
Just a girl spinning lots of plates,
so fast the pies now fly.

I AM A BALLOON

I am a balloon,
I blow hot,
I blow cold,
I am a balloon,
I react with your hot air.
You are full of it.
I inflate with your attention,
I deflate when you deflate,
and I soar and hit the clouds,
when your lips touch mine.

BLACK EYE BOB

Black Eye Bob's been locked up in the think
tank,
no one to thank,
as he was made to walk the plank,
with the rest of the pirates shouting "Black Eye
Bob!"
He's been secretly pining for somewhere else,
a shadow of his former self,
as he dives deep into the ocean,
he's fine,
he knows the motion,
and a mermaid comes to his aid.
He's now absorbed in her potion.
Eloped they dive down deep,
with a whisp of her tail,
she takes Black Eye Bob on the most beautiful
sail,
and they create whirlpools together.
Black Eye Bob hope's it's a dream that will last
forever,
and he wakes up on a sandbank,
with a mermaid to thank.

GRAN

To be that violin player,
or that harp playing angel.
Speak those Gaelic poems and know those fairy-
tales from far,
you taught me this.
As I watched you eat your oatcakes,
you drank your whisky pure.
This has always been you.
I remember the scenery I have always seen with
you,
fields, mountains and waterfalls too.
This has always been you.
I remember your musky candlelit caravan,
You gave me amazing art,
traditional and true,
this has always been you,
fields, waterfalls, poems, fairy-tales and oatcakes
and whisky too,
thanks for the pen,
teaching me to write before I wrote.

A LONG NIGHT ALONE

A long night alone,
sitting by the telephone,
hoping you would call.
But you never called at all.
Wishing you were near me,
closer than that,
making love on a sheepskin mat.
You would hold me tight,
we would kiss all night,
we might fight.
We could be all right,
it would be fine,
we could have a great time.
For a moment I forgot,
you're not mine.

MY POWERS ARE WEAK, I MUST HAVE THE FLU

A cough and a splutter,
a sneeze,
an achoo,
a hanky,
a Lemsip,
and Anadin too,
a hot toddie,
a bath,
bed early for you,
that's how to get rid of a bad ACHOO!!

HUSH HUSH

Psst Psst
Hush hush,
whisper whisper,
hear me softly whispering this to you,
a secret message a private game,
if everyone knows it won't be the same.
A quiet voice,
not a loud shout,
don't let them hear all round about,
a quiet voice,
a fly little whisper,
like a tiptoe,
shhhh,
don't let anyone know.

CYBER FRIEND

U wanna be my cyber friend,
Me & U,
we'll be friends 4eva.
Ah...It's so sweet,
I might not even know you if I passed you on the
street.
We could talk for years,
introduce each other to our cyber peers.
You've got such a pretty face,
I've got double D boobs and a thong of lace.
What star sign are you?
WOW,
Jings,
we're into the same things.
Did you check my nudie pics,
I put them there for you,
use them to wank over if you want to.

BITCHASS BIT OF CLASS EXPERIENCE

SLAM oh SLAM,
Pressure at the Arches,
you are Glasgow's two main men.
And SOMA,
what a record label,
keep rocking me out my coma.
Optimo's pure funk and full of spunk.
Tresor is one of the best,
I must make it there,
whilst FUSE in Brussels,
I've seen your sign,
at I love techno with techno so fine.
From the likes of Ellen Alien and Apparat,
personal favourites of mine.
To seeing MOTOR and KRAFTWERK,
The highlight of my party time.
Dave Clarke,
Two days, two countries in a row — Amsterdam
Dance Event and I Love Techno — jolly good
show!
Octave One, we've had some fun, you brothers
rock my intense brain,
True to form you rocked Amsterdams Melkweg
and Glasgow's Sub Club the same.
Scratch Master Kentaro, what a star, genius I'm
sure,
I watched him drop that needle on the record and

my body hit the floor.
Phil Kieran,
he inspires me no end,
he rocks my body every time, his tunes are immense.
And who would have thought you could be sentimental about Alloy Mental; I AM I AM!
Funk D Void, it's a tough one, I'm stuck with him it's true.
International man of mystery I have muchos respect for you!
A knowledgeable man, Felix the Housecat, only once have I seen,
but we've shared a smile and endless pleasure behind the silver screen.
Andrew Weatherall, Radioactive Man,
down to earth and synthcere,
I love your twisted beats; it brings music to my ear.
Magda at Minus at Pressure,
What a kicking set she plays,
I'm all for female DJ's,
I DJ myself on some days.
Miss Kittin, Golden Boy, The Hacker, with electro you rule,
I once fell in love to Rippin Kittin at Glasgow Art School.
Audion, Mathew Dear, I'm not sure what to say here but this shouldn't be weird,
but your minimal beats are damn fine, thank you for being a silent friend of mine.
Ralph Lawson, he knows my previous,

He's seen it first hand, he tried to stop me getting
thrown out by the bouncers for reasons I still don't
understand.
Green Velvet, you kick ass, at the Carling Academy
you made my birthday first class.
Squarepusher, how fast you move your fingers on
the bass,
You had everyone at Glasgow Art School, dancing
and jumping all-round the place.
Juan Atkins can tell a story, and his music spins me
round, just like a record baby I do like your sound.
Red Planet, again at Glasgow School of Art, I'm a
loyal supporter of this record label right from the
start.
Robert Hood, you're so fucking good!
Theo Parish in the house, on the couch, thank you
my friend.
Jim Masters, you are a master, and we've both been
plastered together, thank you my brother.
Silicone Soul, I know your history, almost from day
one, and you know mine, we've had some fun.
Pete Heller, Alex Paterson of the Orb, Farley Jack
Master Funk, Subculture's very own Dominic and
Harry,
my greatest music experiences are glittery and starry!

MUSICAL SEXUAL ROMANCE

Why does the DJ not dance?
But spins records like they're making musical
sexual romance?
Pumping that DJ desk like they're so turned on in
bed,
but the DJ doesn't dance,
the DJ makes musical sexual romance.
So why does the DJ not dance,
but most certainly grooves,
sways a little,
like a DJ does,
but busts no moves,
makes musical sexual romance?
Musical wanking at its best,
like they're so turned on in bed.
I'm interested to watch,
but they don't dance,
it's not to say they can't,
give the DJ a chance,
they are so good at this musical sexual romance!
Does it take a DJ out of their comfort zone
to be out from behind the desk?
Can the DJ dance like they're so turned on in
bed?
Can they bust some moves?
Pull some shapes on the dancefloor,
but then who's going to DJ and make musical
sexual romance?
Maybe that's why the DJ doesn't dance.

BANKERS

You see what they want you to see,
the ones who think they control you and me.
The puppeteers,
the men with strings,
those who wear the pinkie rings.
The knights of the round table,
those who keep our world "stable."
The men in suits with polished boots,
counting cash to distribute.
Chauffer driven,
shielded from the rain,
never felt a pine of pain.
The aristocrats,
the top cats,
the men who wear top hats,
with gout and shiny red nose,
wife showing off their manicured toes,
that's where all the money goes.

A SCRAPBOOK

Thinking of dry pressing my white roses and
keeping them forever.
A memory of harder times,
Community spirit,
And when people pulled together.
I'm thinking I'll make a scrap book,
Get an instant camera,
Take photos of faces and places,
And signatures,
Pictures,
Postcards,
And love letters,
Because I get so many love letters.
I'll draw pictures of love hearts in red ink,
And arrows in black,
I'll keep random phone numbers there too,
Boys I'm avoiding and don't want to call back.
I'll have sweet wrappers of my favourites,
Club tickets and posters,
Fancy hotels cards I've stayed at,
Old passport stamps from my extinct passports of
places I've visited,
And wine labels I've enjoyed.
I'll have fabrics,
And wall papers,
bits and bobs,
And a diary of friends and frenemies,
I want a bible of memories.

IT'S NO SURPRISE.

It's all gone boom.
Bang goes the toon.
Another lockdown looms.
And I've got the fear,
It's been some year.
Moving into another tier.
Moving into another restriction.
Isolation on prescription.
Mental health problems rise,
It's no surprise.
Anxiety looks in everyone's eyes.
Uncertain what the future looks like,
Waiting on a miracle vaccine.
Or miracle drugs.
Trusting a government untrustworthy,
Looking like financial thugs.
Rich profiting,
The poor suffering,
The sick demise,
As we watch the wealthy rise.
It's no surprise.
Anxiety looks in everyone's eyes.
The lonesome are lonelier,
The boredom is boringer.
Groundhog Day,
Set on repeat play.
With no sign of the virus going away.

And we sit and watch Brexit as we exit,
With our plates already full of stress,
The hungry go hungrier,
It's no surprise.
Anxiety looks in everyone's eyes.

GAMBLING

Gambling away the giro
better pissing it down the pottery,
than throwing it down the slottery.
Losing all your money,
as runny as honey,
a never-ending battle to win back what you've
rattled.
You stay away from certain things because you
know they are addictive,
yet you add another vice to your belt,
it's not funny how losing all your money can be so
seductive.
Where money has no value,
you win,
you lose,
you're up,
you are down,
yet you still go to bed that night after moving your
money from your savings account.
You don't even notice how much you have spent,
or how much time has went.
It's a double whammy,
when time is money and money is time,
You've wasted the afternoon gambling away the
giro bill,
chasing the gambling thrill,
like you've got time to kill,
money to kill.

IRONY, SATIRE AND SARCASM

Irony says sarcasm is fake,
and sarcasm says irony lacks creativity,
while satire will expose your own stupidity.
Irony will always revel in what you didn't expect to
happen,
and sarcasm says you got what you deserved, but
only silently.
Satire will make a joke of you blatantly.
While irony laughs at the weather.
Satire will slag the weather man off to his face and
laugh with no disgrace,
while sarcasm will jest that the weather man is
always right, when he's made a mistake.
Satire will use exaggerated language,
mocking righteous behaviour as a target,
sarcasm will call a dunderhead clever,
the irony is they are all different but are
categorised together.

THIS PLACE IS NUCLEAR

They say the nuclear reactors are unsafe,
The seas of our land potentially in the future an
unsafe place,
Scotland a dumping ground for nuclear waste.
Cracking in the reactors,
Faults found being ignored,
Everywhere the nuclear power is stored.
And the danger underrated,
They would see Glasgow & Edinburgh evacuated.
Due to radioactive contamination,
If the worst does come to the worst,
The only solution to the pollution would be
evacuation of a nation.
The whole of the central belt of Scotland,
And all its beauty,
Doomed to a nuclear future,
The eery quiet streets of Edinburgh,
The standstill of our industrial Glasgow,
Our fields where things used to grow,
Soil spoiled by greed,
People unable to feed from the land,
Or walk on our once beautiful clean sands,
And in their words, I quote,
"Hot graphite could become exposed to air,"
They talk,
But do they care?

MEANT TO BE

Coincidence,
a statistic that is overlooked,
a freak encounter that leaves you spooked.
A moment of serendipity,
a stroke of unexplainable spontaneity.
Two paths that cross,
on a road that's lost,
a chance encounter,
an unplanned event,
I can't explain how I finished your sentence for
you,
I just knew how your story went.
Psychic feelings or just in tune,
predicting the future,
two different countries but still looking at the same
moon.
Dimensions twisted to bring us together,
did a bird just fly by or is that a random feather?
I'm sure I dreamt of you last night,
and my own personal favourite,
if it rhymes it must be right.
Have I been here before or is this deja vu?
I have a strong sense of familiarity with something
I never knew.

A GLASGOW BAR

I'm in a Glasgow bar,
old drunk men calling me hen,
ordering their whisky chasers and then ordering
them again and again.
Maggie puts on the juke box Country Roads,
while the barmaid pours four shots as the
businessmen in suits make a toast.
The owner of the bar sits at the end counting his
books,
and wee Lucy's eyeing up the talent,
she regularly eyes up anyone in boots.
Old Jim's had too much to drink and someone
needs to take him home,
so, the barmaid calls him a taxi on her mobile
phone.
There's a family in wetting their new baby's head,
and there's empty glasses and a paper sitting where
a man earlier read.
And there's me,
after having a drink or three,
sat on a bar stool,
writing poetry.

A FAIR AND FRANK EXCUSE

It's a confusing affair,
And it's sometimes unfair,
And it's fair to say I'll do it anyway.
When suddenly,
you're left feeling a bit Frank Sinatra-esque,
he done it his way.
When he was writing his song,
I bet at some point he thought the same,
I'll do it anyway,
because it's a confusing affair,
and it's sometimes unfair.
But fair to say,
I'm going to do it anyway,
and if I ever need an excuse,
I'll use this one and I'll say,
"I did it my way."

GUILT

You're not always right
I'm guilty of thinking that I am right,
but so are you,
and I'm not guilty of that with you,
cos you're too busy being the right one.
I watch you argue your point,
dictate your opinion,
and push your views.
And when someone questions you,
you're still always right.

THE BEST FRUIT OF ALL

The orange is bitter,
the apple is sweet,
but you are the juiciest peach I ever did eat.
You are a ripe banana,
as I peel back your skin,
you are the pear of the pack,
that I WILL NEVER put back.
Sour grape will never do,
I could make a fine wine with you!
A firm melon,
with a fine seed,
you are the honey to my mead.

WILD HORSE

Your horse looks like it's never been trekked,
all brand new and well hoofed,
shining coat and well groomed.
Active but yet so inactive.
Attractive.
Is your horse a show horse?
Your horse looks like it's never been whipped,
never kicked,
never ripped up a moor.
never tripped on a mountain's ledge,
you look like you were never scared of falling off
the ledge with your horse.
Your horse looks nameless,
and shameless,
and completely blameless to any foul play,
your horse looks tame and not wild,
never bore its own child,
never eaten hay with a stray horse,
your horse looks like it's never been trekked.

ARMAGEDDON

The earth shook and no one knew why,
volcanoes erupted,
and heavy raindrops fell down from the sky.
there were forest fires,
the waters rose,
the hottest lands got hotter,
and where was cold no longer froze.
The earth hit drought,
the animals suffered,
the people grew hungry,
and life was challenged,
as the world faced a universal famine.
The air grew thick,
carbon monoxide rose,
landscapes empty where trees once grew.
Vultures scoured the skies,
hunting death with their beaks and eyes,
bees that flew no longer flys.
Flowers were a thing of the past,
sand sits where once was grass.
Whirlwinds soared,
and tsunamis roared,
flooding towns and leaving villages floored.
The banks all burst,
The dams grew weak,
The power cables did not function in the streets.
The people grew scared,

and looted goods,
Stealing and crime in their neighbourhoods.

I CALL IT SELFIE EVOLUTION

All these selfies are changing the way we smile,
they are giving us pose lines on our smile lines,
they are giving us wrinkles on our crinkles,
changing the way we mingle,
with each other,
a selfie to a lover.
If the wind changes,
our faces will forever face the left-hand side,
our best side,
our best angle.
With our eyes flattering,
forever a picture of pride.
Our selfie faces adopted by our children,
as young as three,
posing like you and me.
Seductively glancing,
pouting and pooching,
winking and acting cool,
mouths wide open showing our tonsils in pictures
of fun,
saying look at me,
look at everyone.
Beautiful people.
Evolving with technology,
losing the art of speech and relying on the language
of the body,
relying on vanity.

At the same time, making everyone feel beautiful, but does it?

PASSION

You know, the word comes from the Greek verb,
meaning to suffer.
A strong feeling about a person or thing,
one has passion for their lover.
A compelling emotion,
emotion with enthusiasm.
The best orgasm.
An intense inclination.
An infinity of positive vibrations.
Sometimes makes it impossible to listen to reason.
Passion is a feeling.
Hamlet once said, "Give me the man that is not
passion's slave, and I shall wear him in my heart's
core."
Intellectual passions increase our motivation and if
we're lucky our occupation.
It affects how we function,
a physical, intellectual and mental conjunction.
The more passion there is, the better the poetry!

YOU NEVER KNOW YOUR LUCK

You never know your luck,
But you know when luck has struck.
You might find a tenner in a taxi,
Or a free ride on the train,
You might meet the man on your dreams in a
different country,
And bump into him again.

You never know your luck,
But you know when luck has struck.
You might not think you'll win the lottery,
But you still throw in your buck.
Serendipity,
Coincidence,
Or pure fate alone,
Should all be things to place your confidence in,
You never know who will win.

You never know your luck,
But you know when luck has struck.

IMAGINE

Imagine not looking at the horizon straight on,
possibly the horizon is situated to the right,
maybe you need to look back on the horizon.
Imagine looking at the horizon in a different
direction.
We always look out to the horizon.
Maybe we need to look into it.

GROWING OLD

Growing old is hard I'm told,
it's only going get worse I'm told.
Life goes downhill when you get old,
or so I'm told.
At an early age I watched my family go grey,
At an early age I started to pray,
Please God, please no greys.
Growing old is no laughing matter,
or so I'm told,
and telling me that doesn't make the situation any
better,
growing old is not fun,
well, jeezo,
think I'll give this growing old a good run.
Growing old makes your bones creak,
or so I'm told,
I keep repeating this line because there is no way
I'm admitting to growing old.
You can't go out for three-night benders when your
growing old,
or so I'm told.
The hangovers are worse and you need more
sleep,
when you're growing old,
or so I'm told.
Growing old is a gift,
I hope we all grow old.

A QUICK POEM

Stuck in this prison of mobile activity,
Fingertips scratching the glass screen,
Trying to get closer and further away.
It's the same as it's ever been,
But an attempt to break free might break me.

LOST WORDS IN THE WRITER'S MIND

Lost words in the writer's mind,
words even the writer is scared to find,
so, you might not understand this one,
but try, because it could be fun,
but I don't know what I will find,
lost words missing in the writer's mind.

ART, WHAT IT'S ALL ABOUT?

Art is not a competition,
blessed as we who create additions,
to the world in any art form,
through art we take the world by storm.
Pick up that pencil pen and paint,
draw a story with words that's just insane,
get creative with your melodic beats,
spray paint your art in the street.
Dance until your heart's content,
use your art as a vent.

WAITING

I keep expecting to see you,
I thought I'd have seen you long before now.
And still I wait to meet you.
Is it true you stood me up?
The girls seem to think so, but I know you better
than that.
I would not be waiting for a guy who stands me up.
I'll wait as long as it takes,
But you do know it's rude to keep a girl waiting.

YOUR DREAMS ARE ON SHOW

Your dreams are on show,
People see your darkest nightmares everywhere
they go,
Your ambitious colour pastel painted twilight,
On show every night,
Your dusted down decorations that dangle and
twinkle are out to mingle.
Mr Sandman is getting more friends due to how
much you have out him on display,
the minions you dreamt last night have come out
to play.
Your fairy-tale castle is being built on the island
you only dreamed up last week.
And as you didn't wash your face this morning you
still have fairy dust sprinkles on your cheek.
Your black and white dreams that don't exist still
don't exist,
and the dreams you forgot are in full progress and
clunking away in the background,
your handsome prince has been found,
not once but twice,
China now has more rice fields,
due to the dreams you so perfectly wield.
Inventions and creations are in full celebration.
Sleep well tonight.

ABOUT CARLA

Carla Woodburn is a poet who was born in Inverness. She was raised in Tain in the Highlands of Scotland and currently resides in Clydebank, where she has now been longer than the Highlands.

Carla studied Business Administration, Event Management and Social Care in different colleges around the central belt. She has been writing since her school days, expressing everyday situations through poetry.

Carla moved to Barcelona in 2011 where she lived for four years, joined a poetry group called The Poetry Workshop and jointly with the group published an anthology 'Together Apart'. Carla has five poems published in this anthology.

Moving back to Glasgow at the end of 2015 Carla joined the Glasgow spoken word scene, and found Tell It Slant poetry bookshop, (the only bookshop in Scotland dedicated to poetry) where she started her own monthly poetry event named Express Yourself and became a trustee of the bookshop. She quickly became acquainted with Sunny Govan Radio and took Express Yourself to the airwaves with her own successful weekly poetry radio show also called Express Yourself, which she still runs to this day. Carla is part of a poetry collective named Woman With Fierce Words, with whom she has been published in the anthology 'Woman With Fierce Words'.

Carla was approached by the Scots Language Centre in 2020 and invited to take on the role of Scots Poetry Editor and facilitate an online Scots Poetry Column featuring a new Scots poet every month, Carla is still committed to this role today. Carla takes part in many spoken word events, festivals and open mic nights around Scotland and enjoys sharing poetry with others.